Dee Kids

(Hunting and Fishing Books for Kids)

By

Isiah Maxwell

© Copyright 2018
All rights reserved.

The content contained within this book may not be reproduced, duplicated or transmitted without direct written permission from the author or the publisher.

Under no circumstances will any blame or legal responsibility be held against the publisher, or author, for any damages, reparation, or monetary loss due to the information contained within this book. Either directly or indirectly.

Legal Notice:

This book is copyright protected. This book is only for personal use. You cannot amend, distribute, sell, use, quote or paraphrase any part, or the content within this book, without the consent of the author or publisher.

Disclaimer Notice:

Please note the information contained within this document is for educational and entertainment purposes only. All effort has been executed to present accurate, up to date, and reliable, complete information. No warranties of any kind are declared or implied. Readers acknowledge that the author is not engaging in the rendering of legal, financial, medical or professional advice. The content within this book has been derived from various sources. Please consult a licensed professional before attempting any techniques outlined in this book.

By reading this document, the reader agrees that under no circumstances is the author responsible for any losses, direct or indirect, which are incurred as a result of the use of information contained within this document, including, but not limited to, — errors, omissions, or inaccuracies.

Table Of Contents

Introduction 7

Chapter 1-Why Hunting is Fun 9

  Reasons Why Deer Hunting is Fun 10

    You Discover More about Nature 10
    You Spend More Time with Your Family and Friends 10
    Deer Camps are Great! 11
    More Bonding Time with Parents 12
    Time to Get a Deer Skin Glove and Beautiful Knife Handles 13
    Deer Meat is So Delicious! 13
    Experience Culture and Tradition in 3D 14

Chapter 2 – Equipment to Bring 16

  What You Need to Bring on Your Hunting trip 16

    Rubber-Soled Boots 17
    Backpacks 18
    Scent Block 18
    Binoculars 19
    Pocket Knife 19
    Hunting Rifles 20
    Compound Bows 21
    Water Bottles 21
    Headlamp 22
    Hunting Clothes 22
    Survival Kit 22
    Hunting Documents and License 23
    Trail camera 23
    Food 24

Chapter 3-Tips and Tricks 25
Cover Your Scent 25
Use Deer Perfume 26
Use Deer Mating Calls 27
Stay Quiet 27
Practice Your Shooting Skills 28
Try Going Deeper Into the Woods 28
Know Where and When to Hunt 29
Follow a Blood Trail 30
Bring Enough Warm Clothes and Your Best Sleeping Bag 31
Always Hang Your Kill 31
Watch Out for Predators 32

Chapter 4- Safety Measures 33
Wear an Orange Outfit 33
Always Point the Muzzle of Your Rifle in a Safe Direction 34
Be Sure of Your Target 35
Don't Shoot at Flat Hard Surfaces 35
Don't Climb a Tree or Fence with a Loaded Gun . 36
Know Your Safe Zone 36
Use a Full Body Safety Harness When Climbing Trees 37
Take a GPS or Compass 37

Watch Out for Slippery and Sharp Surfaces 38
Chapter 5- Wildlife Conservation 39
  Facts about Wildlife Conservation 40
  How to Learn More about Wildlife Conservation .41
    Watch documentaries and read books 42
    Visit natural habitats in your area 42
Glossary 44

Introduction

Autumn is drawing near – it is finally hunting season. The hunting dates have been posted and you are filled with a lot of questions. Perhaps, this is your first hunting trip and you are excited and also scared on how to go about it. You are probably thinking if it's better to stay indoors and watch your favorite TV shows or play a game. Don't give up just yet. Hold on and take a deep breath. You are about to experience the best moments of your life.

This is the time when you climb up the ranks to start big game hunting. Although the thought of spending long hours in the woods while waiting for a deer is quite daunting, I assure you that every minute or hour spent tracking your quarry is worth it.

Yes, the excitement you feel at that moment when you finally sight your prey and take the shot is the reward. Mind you, deer hunting is more than just shooting down deer; it is also an opportunity to appreciate the value of life. So, get ready to be welcomed into the age-old tradition of deer hunting. Prepare your mind as we introduce you to the basics, tricks, and tips of deer hunting.

Chapter 1-Why Hunting is Fun

Getting wet, getting hungry, cold, and scared while waiting for your deer to get within range is a common experience in hunting. Sometimes, you must endure ticks and mosquitoes on a hot and sticky summer afternoon while hanging stands and checking trail cameras. To some, this is not their idea of fun. I guess you are probably nodding your head in agreement right now. Well, you should know that there are two types of fun. Sounds cheesy, right? Let me explain. The first type of fun is that which you enjoy in that moment. This type of fun includes doing activities such as jet skiing, going to the movies with friends, and playing games. The second type of fun might seem tiring in that moment. For example, when you are hunting a mature buck. However, when you look back on those moments you realize that you wouldn't trade them for the world. And that, my friend, is the definition of fun. What's more? There are a thousand reasons why deer hunting is fun. So, here are a few to start with.

Reasons Why Deer Hunting is Fun

You Discover More about Nature

As a deer hunter, you know more about nature than non-hunters will ever know. You get to discover your role in maintaining the circle of life. Yes, your job as a hunter is to maintain the population of the deer herd. Your understanding of wild places is more than any school degree can offer you.

You Spend More Time with Your Family and Friends

Deer hunting is just the perfect activity if you want

to build lasting and beautiful memories with your loved ones. Hunting season offers you the opportunity to bond with your family members and friends. Heck! It's more interesting when you hunt together with family. You can also bring your friends along on such family trips. Besides, learning one or two tricks from your parents or guardians is a great way of knowing more about deer hunting. Perhaps, you will get lucky and snag a big whitetail. In addition to this, you will have people to help you drag your first kill to the camp.

Deer Camps are Great!

Summer camps are great places to have fun and meet new people. Well, deer camps are more fun. You just can't compare the fun you have in summer camps with deer camps. Deer camps were once for men only. In recent years, however, more women are joining deer camps. So, there's no restriction on who can join deer camps. You will have the opportunity to meet new friends with similar interests and also gain more experience in shooting down deer. So, don't hesitate to have fun while visiting deer camps.

More Bonding Time with Parents

Most of your childhood revolves around busy class schedules and pressing games consoles. These activities take up most of your time and leave you with less time with your parents. Heck! You only get to talk more with your parents at the weekend. So, why don't you spend those precious moments doing an activity you both love? Fathers can share their hunting experiences and tricks with their sons or daughters. In addition to this, you will learn a deep appreciation for life and the fact that death is inevitable. What's more, the memories you glean from these moments will stay with you all your life.

Time to Get a Deer Skin Glove and Beautiful Knife Handles

You will never forget your first knife, especially if the handle is made from the antlers of a buck that you killed. Deer antlers have a strong and smooth texture that make it the perfect material for knife handles. Mature bucks shed their antlers around mid-December to February and grow new ones. So you can also come across discarded antlers while hunting for deer. What's more, it gives you bragging rights amongst your peers. In addition to this, you can also turn in your deer hides to a hide processing industry and they will give you beautiful deerskin gloves in return. Remember, you can always flaunt your deerskin gloves to your friends and peers.

Deer Meat is So Delicious!

You are missing out if you have never tasted deer meat. Also called venison, deer meat is cleaner and healthier than most of your store-bought meat products. It's completely organic and comes with lots of nutrients. Most importantly, venison tastes so good. Its rich stringy taste will leave a lasting memory in your mind.

Experience Culture and Tradition in 3D

Let me ask you this question - do you know how much art and culture has been created about deer hunting? Well, I don't, but I do know that it's a lot. Deer hunting has inspired lots of paintings, novels, and even cultures. For example, the Native American culture revolves around hunting and the use of animal products to make different materials. Thousands of deer paintings from the Stone Age all the way up to modern times are being displayed in different museum galleries all around the world. Yes, hunting is a noble duty that is passed from generation to generation. So, when next you hold that rifle or crossbow, do it with pride as you are about to participate in an activity as old as time. Let your blaze orange clothes proclaim your love for hunting.

Chapter 2 – Equipment to Bring

First impression matters in hunting. Kids will definitely love hunting if the first time is fun and exciting. Comfort, fun, and success on the field will build your kids' interest in hunting. For this reason, parents and guardians have to ensure that they procure good hunting equipment for their wards.

The success of your hunting trip depends on your essential hunting gear. In fact, your survival in the wild depends on it. From energy bars to water bottles to knives to rifles and bows, these items matter a lot. Sometimes, you might find yourself stranded and these items will help you to survive the wild.

What You Need to Bring on Your Hunting trip

Before you hit the hunting gear store with your kids, you should know that not all hunting gear is built for young ones. Sometimes, the specification of adult hunting gear is different from that of kids. For instance, handing an adult rifle to a child can lead to a lot of unpleasant experiences. So, take a look at the list of hunting equipment that will make your hunt a success.

Rubber-Soled Boots

You definitely don't want to be walking barefoot through the thick forest. Therefore, you need a pair of thick rubber-soled boots to protect your feet from blisters and the cold. Remember, always go for high-quality boots if you don't want blisters on your feet. Furthermore, rubber-soled boots are great for deer hunting. Deer have a high sense of smell and they get agitated when they smell human scent. Therefore, it's best to get a rubber-soled boot since it doesn't retain smell, unlike leather-soled boots. In addition to this, always choose a lightweight boot since you don't want to delay the rest of your hunting team.

Backpacks

Here's equipment that can either shorten your hunting trip or make it memorable. In the woods, you rely more on your backpack since it contains your survival kits. From housing water bottles to maps to trail cameras to energy bars, backpacks play an important role in hunting. Therefore, getting a good backpack should be at the top of your list. Look for a backpack that is light, has a waist strap, and good padding for comfort.

Scent Block

Do you remember when I said deer have an excellent sense of smell? Well, here's an interesting fact - deer have a better sense of smell than dogs. So, you should avoid spraying your favorite body spray when going on a deer hunt.

The best option is to spray a scent killer or block on your clothes and gear. Scent blocks mask your scent from being detected by deer. This was why we advised you to wear rubber-soled boots since they help to absorb the scent block.

Binoculars

Every hunter should have binoculars. This device helps you to view your prey at a distance without getting close enough to scare it away. In fact, most people use binoculars to gauge the distance of their prey, before using the scope on the rifle. Your binoculars must have a high magnification and must be lightweight.

Pocket Knife

Here's a useful hunting implement. A combo set with a fillet knife and a gut hook is preferable. Some hunting knives come with a hard nylon sheath to protect you from accidental cuts. So, ensure that you sheath your knives at all times.

Hunting Rifles

Well, we've come to the important part: hunting rifles. Hunting rifles are every hunter's best friend. These rifles are good for shooting down prey. With the aid of a good scope, you can easily shoot down a whitetail several yards away. Yes, it is important that every beginner or child starts with a rifle before trying to use a bow. There are many hunting rifles available for children in gun stores.

You can start with an Ar-15 collapsible stock for children between 6 and 10 years old. The total gun weight should not be more than 6½ pounds. Kids above 12 years old can easily handle an AR bolt-action rifle. Furthermore, take your kids along when you want to buy a hunting rifle for them. Ensure they are comfortable with the rifle before buying it.

Compound Bows

I'd advise kids to learn how to shoot properly with a rifle before using a hunting bow. However, you can also start with the compound bow if your kid has shown an interest in archery. Compound bows come in different sizes. So, parents are advised to pick the ones they can easily shoot with.

Water Bottles

You don't know how long you will stay in the woods. So, it's important to always keep a water bottle with you to prevent dehydration. You always put the water bottle at the top of your list. Additionally, bring along some iodine tablets and a compact water filter in case you run out of water and you need to refill your water bottle from a nearby pond or stream.

Headlamp

This device might come in handy when you are looking for your way back home. Many hunters have lost their way in the woods because they have no headlamp. You should know that headlamps are not really effective for hunting deer at night. Deer are very active at night and they will run away if you point a headlamp at them.

Hunting Clothes

In some states, hunters are required to always wear a blaze orange outfit whenever they are in the woods. This will alert other hunters of their presence. However, you need camouflage apparel if you want to blend in with the environment.

Survival Kit

So many things can go wrong in the woods and it's

important to always have a survival kit with you. Your survival kit should have all the latest survival tools. It should contain matches, ibuprofen, compass, first-aid kit, and blister kit

Hunting Documents and License

You need a license before you can hunt in a state. Ensure you have all the necessary documents before going on a deer hunt or else you will be fined by the authorities.

Trail camera

This is a remote camera used to track game over long periods of time. Since you can follow your prey constantly, the trail camera will use motion-detection sensors to gauge when large animals have passed. The sensors will create an image with time and date, and the hunters will be able to use these images to plan their hunting patterns. It is important for you to buy a sturdy and waterproof trail camera. This will allow you to place them in the wild for a long time.

Food

You need food if you are going to stay in the wild for a long time. Therefore, you should fill your backpack with protein and energy bars, fruits and fruit snacks Be sure to avoid bringing anything with meat scent such as beef jerky, since the scent might attract predators and scare off your prey.

There is so much hunting gear that I did not include in the list above. However, I have made sure to include the essential tools that will help make your hunting trip easier. Mind you, you need shelter and warm clothing if you are going to stay overnight in the wild.

Chapter 3-Tips and Tricks

Deer hunting can be quite interesting and fun. However, the interesting and fun part is for those who have discovered the secrets of deer hunting. Sometimes, you see hunters loading as much as five kills on their truck. You also see many hunters go home without a kill every day of the hunting season. So, what is the secret? What makes some hunters successful while others are not? To be a successful hunter, you need more than hunting equipment to get your prey. Yes, it is necessary for you to discover the tricks successful hunters use to get their prey. Furthermore, your deer hunting experience will become interesting and fun if you discover the tips and tricks. Let's check out some of the tricks used in deer hunting

Cover Your Scent

This is one of the most important rules of deer hunting. A deer can smell your scent from over a mile away. Yes, their sense of smell is that great. Deers can smell the scent you leave on the ground and in the air. The ability to completely cover your scent will determine if your hunting seasons will be great or not. The good news is that you can buy scent block soaps or blocks to remove your scent. This will help you to track deer without spooking them.

Use Deer Perfume

Often, successful hunters use deer perfume to attract deer. You should know that this is not like the nice-smelling perfume you spray on your body. Deer perfume includes any substance that you can use to attract deer. For instance, hunters use a drag rag in doe estrous to attract bucks during mating season. However, this method is only limited to the mating season. Therefore, you should include other deer "perfumes" like deer urine, deer feed, and deer feeders.

Use Deer Mating Calls

You can also dupe the deer by rattling antlers to get its attention. Some hunters use a special whistle that mimics different calls to attract deer.

Stay Quiet

You have to watch every step you take when hunting deer. Deer have excellent hearing. So, covering your scent is not enough to hide your presence. In fact, deer can easily hear your movements from a mile away. In addition to this, it takes them about 2 hours to return if they hear your movements. Remember, the wilderness is not your marching ground. Every step has to be taken with care. Set up your hunting stand a day or two before hunting day - this will help to minimize the noise you make. You can also try quick-stepping. Try taking quick steps in a short sprint for up to 20 yards. Remember to always take light steps.

Practice Your Shooting Skills

It is difficult to shoot down a deer if you don't have enough practice shooting. Try to visit a gun range with your parents or guardians. This will prepare you for the recoil and the loud noise of gunfire. If you are using a bow, try to find one that is perfect for you. A good hunting weapon should be light and easy to handle. So, try to perfect your shooting skills before you go on a hunt.

Try Going Deeper Into the Woods

Here's a secret tip for those hunting with a large group. Large hunting groups create noise that sends deer far away from their range. The best thing is to stray away from the group and follow your own trail. You stand a higher chance of sighting a deer group in a place with little disturbance. Don't forget to bring your compass and map if you decide to move deeper into the woods.

Know Where and When to Hunt

This tip will save you a lot of disappointment. Deer are usually active at sunset and in the early morning. This means that the best time to hunt is in the evening as the sun sets and very early in the morning. For morning hunts, you have to wake up very early and set up camp on the deer's route to bedding. Additionally, you should set up camp around the deer feeding area at sunset. However, this strategy doesn't work every time. You can hunt at any time of the day if you are in the rut season.

You can't just start hunting in an area without knowing the movement of the animals in the area. Therefore, it is important to scout an area before hunting season. Deer need to feed, defecate, and mate. Your job is to know where and when the deer do all these things. This will help you to choose the ideal hunting location. By tracing deer droppings and trails, you will be able to understand their pattern.

Follow a Blood Trail

Don't expect your prey to fall immediately after you shoot at it. It takes a while for a deer to die after you've shot it. They mostly leave a blood trail once wounded. So, move quietly as you track the blood trail of your quarry. Have patience and quietly observe every blood spot you come across. If you notice that the blood spots are frothy, then your shot pierced the heart or the lungs of the deer. This means your deer won't be alive for much longer and your chase is nearly over. One more thing: watch out for animals that drop at the shot. Most times, the deer might fall from shock, then recover and run away. So, get ready to fire another shot or arrow at the animal if it drops instantly.

Bring Enough Warm Clothes and Your Best Sleeping Bag

It is going to be very cold at night and very early in the morning. Ensure that you bring warm clothes. If you are staying in the woods all through the night, you can bring a woodstove to warm you and your hunting partners. Also, don't forget to bring along your best sleeping bag on your hunting trip.

Always Hang Your Kill

Predators like coyotes and grizzly bears can quickly consume your kill. So, try to hang the carcass about 3 feet above ground level. Hang the carcass if you shoot a deer late in the evening, if you can't drag it to your van. Make camp in an area where you can easily view your kill. Quietly leave if you see a grizzly munching on the carcass.

Watch Out for Predators

You are not the only predator out there in the wild. Sometimes, coyotes and bobcats can come close to where you camp. So it's better if you have a shotgun to scare them off. Furthermore, try a different deer call once in a while. Coyotes become accustomed to certain calls.

So, these are the top tricks and tips you need to use in your deer hunts. The tips are so easy to use and understand. So, young hunters don't need to miss out on all the fun of deer hunting.

Chapter 4- Safety Measures

Are you ready to explore and have fun on your hunting trip? Well, wait a minute. Before you start your hunting trip, let me ask you this question - are you familiar with the safety measures of deer hunting? Yes, your safety is very important. Every year, more young hunters join in deer hunting. The woods are filled with anxious hunters, waiting for the perfect opportunity to shoot down their prey. These hunters are so eager to start hunting that they often fail to follow safety measures. Therefore, they end up injuring themselves or others during hunting. So, let's look at the safety measures you need to follow to avoid accidents.

Wear an Orange Outfit

Hunters are required to wear bright orange

clothes in some states. For example, you must wear at least 400 square inches of orange when hunting. This is a safety measure since people have been shot by mistake. It is very easy to mistake a fellow hunter or non-hunter for a deer in the woods. Therefore, the orange cloth will notify other hunters of your presence in that area. It is also important to put on orange headgear. Try not to use clothes that blend with the environment.

Always Point the Muzzle of Your Rifle in a Safe Direction

Never point your rifle in anyone's direction. Furthermore, do not rest your muzzle on your foot. Always assume that your rifle is loaded and never place your hand on the trigger until you are ready o fire. Also, never fire until you are sure that it is a deer. In addition to this, always have the safety on until you are ready to fire at your target.

These safety measures will save your life and those of your families.

Be Sure of Your Target

This is what your binoculars are made for. Identify your target and what is behind and in front of it. Your rifle scope is not enough to verify your target. Always use your binoculars to verify your target before shooting with the aid of your rifle scope. Make sure there are no hunters before or behind your target. Avoid shooting at an animal at the top of a hillside, since you don't know what's on the other side. Lastly, understand how far your bullet or arrow will travel to determine the chances of it hitting a wrong target.

Don't Shoot at Flat Hard Surfaces

Bullets can bounce off rocks and other hard surfaces. So, avoid shooting at flat surfaces.

Remember, your only target is a deer.

Don't Climb a Tree or Fence with a Loaded Gun

You might accidentally shoot yourself if you don't unload your gun while climbing trees or fences.

Know Your Safe Zone

This is a very important safety measure for those hunting in groups. Always keep a distance of 30 to 40 yards between you and the closest hunter when you are hunting in groups. Stay in sight of one another and there should be no more than 3 hunters in a hunting group.

Use a Full Body Safety Harness When Climbing Trees

Tree stands are important in deer hunting. It gives you an aerial view of your surroundings. However, people have gotten injured when they fall off their tree strand. Therefore, it's important to always use a full body harness whenever you use a tree stand.

Take a GPS or Compass

It is possible to get lost while chasing your quarry. Carrying a GPS device or compass will help you to re-trace your steps back to camp. Remember; always have your GPS or compass with you at all times. Lastly, always carry a first-aid kit to treat any injury.

Watch Out for Slippery and Sharp Surfaces

You must watch out for the uneven terrain common in the wild. Sometimes, these terrains are covered with twigs and other materials. So, you never know until you fall down. This mostly occurs in winter when the ground is covered with snow. So, I'd advise walking with a stick to search for sharp surfaces.

Chapter 5- Wildlife Conservation

What will you do if there are no more tigers or lions or penguins in the world anymore? What will you do if you find out that the zoo doesn't have your favorite animals anymore? It is sad, right? There aren't many types of animals in the wild anymore. Although you might find some of them in the zoo, it is difficult to find them in the wild. Yes, these types of animals are called endangered species.

Every year their numbers keep decreasing due to poaching, over-hunting, and the clearing of their natural homes. These animals might become extinct if we are not careful. Therefore, as a deer hunter, it is important for you to learn about wildlife conservation. This will help you to appreciate the role of these animals in the world. You will also learn that deer hunting helps to maintain the balance of the world. Let us take a look at some important things about wildlife conservation.

Facts about Wildlife Conservation

- Animals in different parts of the world can become endangered due to over-hunting, using weed killers that make animals sick.

- Plants can also become endangered.

- We have not discovered all the animals and plants in the world. So, there could be species going extinct before we even know about them.

- The Red List contains the names of thousands of endangered animal and plant species.

- The dodo is an extinct animal that died

hundreds of years ago. It was a bird that couldn't fly. It lived on the island of Mauritius.

- Zoos help to keep animals safe from extinction. Zoo workers help to keep these animals healthy and safe with the hope of returning them to the wild later. You can learn about wildlife conservation by visiting a zoo or an aquarium close to where you live.

- Some of the endangered species in the world include the Siberian tiger, the polar bear, the giant panda, and the right whale.

How to Learn More about Wildlife Conservation

You can try these activities if you want to learn more about wildlife conservation.

Watch documentaries and read books

You cannot learn enough about wildlife conservation from your teachers. To learn more about wildlife conservation, you have to visit the library and look for books about the topic. You can also read books online and watch documentaries.

Visit natural habitats in your area

You can explore the natural areas in your environment with your parents. Tell them to organize treasure hunts for you to take time to observe the birds, bugs, and plants when you follow your parents on hunting trips. All these activities will help you to appreciate nature more.

Here's a fun activity for you - some conservation organizations allow people to adopt endangered animals. This is a fun way to learn about endangered species and also contribute to the organization that protects them. They will send you pictures of your animals and keep you updated on other animals too.

Glossary

Aerial view: this is when you can see your surroundings from a high level.

Autumn: this is the season between summer and winter.

Blood trail: a line of blood made by a wounded animal.

Bobcat: a large cat that lives in North America.

Buck: a male deer

Coyotes: a small wild animal that look like dogs and wolves. They are commonly found in North America.

Dehydration: the process of losing too much water.

Doe estrous: a doe scent that is used to attract bucks.

Doe: a female deer.

Drag rag: a piece of cloth that you apply scent to.

Endangered: animals or plants about to go extinct.

Extinction: The acts of making something die out.

Frothy: contains air bubbles.

Full body harness: a device that helps to protect people from falls.

Grizzly bears: a large and strong bear

Habitat: the place where an animal or plant normally lives or grows.

Humid: a lot of moisture in the air.

Hunting gear: tools used in hunting.

Hunting stand: a platform used by hunters to get a clearer view of their environment.

License: an official document that lets you do something

Light-weight: an object that is not heavy

Magnification: when you make things bigger

Muzzle: the hole at the end of a gun where the bullet comes out.

Poaching: hunting without a license.

Population: the number of people or animals who live in a place.

Predator: an animal that kills other animals for food.

Quarry: prey.

Species: a group of plants or animals that are similar.

Sprint: to run at top speed over a short distance.

Strategy: a careful plan.

The Red List: a complete list of all the animals and plants in the world. It is used to determine which species are endangered.

Venison: deer meat.

Whitetail: North American deer with a tail which is white underneath.

Woodstove: a stove that uses wood for fuel.

Made in the USA
Monee, IL
25 May 2021